Clip-Art Activity Features for Children

Howard Paris, Illustrator

Foreword by George W. Knight

BAKER BOOK HOUSE
Grand Rapids, Michigan 49516

ISBN: 0-8010-7119-4

Printed in the United States of America

Foreword

The typical church newsletter/worship bulletin contains little or nothing directed specifically to the children of the congregation. This book offers a practical answer to this need. It is filled with activities that children from ages 4–9 will enjoy.

Each feature in this collection is ready to use, complete with illustration, activity, instructions, and answer. All you have to do as newsletter editor is clip a feature and paste it down on your newsletter/bulletin layout sheet for reproduction by copying machine, electronic stencil, or offset press.

The creator of these features—Howard Paris—has worked with me in the production of several other clip-art books for Baker Book House. All his work is excellent, but these features for children show him at his very best. Howard understands children, and he knows how to design activities that teach important lessons by appealing to their inquisitive, fun-loving natures.

Let us know how you used these features and how the children responded. This will help us in planning and designing similar books. The address is Baker Book House, P. O. Box 6287, Grand Rapids, MI 49516.

George W. Knight

CROSSWORD!

1.
2.
L
3.
F
4.
O
5.
6.
7.
8.
L
9.

1. Kitten
2. Base----
3. Falls off tree
4. Story----
5. Swing it at ball
6. Goes "Who-o-o"
7. Goes "Oink"
8. Not short
9. Not bad

WORK THE PUZZLE—THEN PUT THE WORDS IN THE DARK COLUMN IN THE PROPER SPACES BELOW

We can always

____ __ ___

about anything

ANSWER: We can always talk to God about anything.

What's the Answer?

1.
2.
3.
4.
5.
6.
7.
TAKE THE FIRST LETTER OF THE WORD THAT DESCRIBES EACH DRAWING—PUT THEM IN THE MATCHING SPACES BELOW!
8.
9.
10.
11.
12.
13.
14.

__ __ should __ __ __ __
(4 6) (12 6 8 10)

our __ __ __ __ __ __ __ __ __
(13 3 1 6 7 11 14) (11 9)

what is __ __ __ __ __
(3 1 5 12 2)

ANSWER: We should help our friends do what is right.

CROSSWORD!

1. Kitten
2. Base____
3. Falls off tree
4. Story____
5. Swing it at ball
6. Goes "Who-o-o"
7. Goes "Oink"
8. Not short
9. Not bad

WORK THE PUZZLE— THEN PUT THE WORDS IN THE DARK COLUMN IN THE PROPER SPACES BELOW

We can always
____ __ ___
about anything

ANSWER: We can always talk to God about anything.

What's the Answer?

TAKE THE FIRST LETTER OF THE WORD THAT DESCRIBES EACH DRAWING—PUT THEM IN THE MATCHING SPACES BELOW!

__ __ should __ __ __ __
(4 6) (12 6 8 10)
our __ __ __ __ __ __ __ __ __
(13 3 1 6 7 11 14) (11 9)
what is __ __ __ __ __
(3 1 5 12 2)

ANSWER: We should help our friends do what is right.

HELP!

Use your pencil to help Tommy find a great Bible truth. Don't cross any lines!

JESUS LOVES ME

Hidden Words!

A	P	B	Q	G	O	D	W	S	I
R	G	R	E	A	T	E	S	T	M
H	B	C	G	I	F	T	D	E	F
J	G	A	I	X	T	O	Z	J	K
W	N	U	S	P	B	U	I	S	W
G	V	K	M	J	E	S	U	S	Y

LOOK LEFT TO RIGHT...

Look for one or more hidden words in each line. Write them in the spaces below and find something we should remember!

___'S __________

_____ ___ ___

___ ______

ANSWER: God's greatest gift to us is Jesus.

HELP!

Use your pencil to help Tommy find a great Bible truth. Don't cross any lines!

JESUS
LOVES
ME

Hidden Words!

A	P	B	Q	G	O	D	W	S	I
R	G	R	E	A	T	E	S	T	M
H	B	C	G	I	F	T	D	E	F
J	G	A	I	X	T	O	Z	J	K
W	N	U	S	P	B	U	I	S	W
G	V	K	M	J	E	S	U	S	Y

LOOK LEFT TO RIGHT...

Look for one or more hidden words in each line. Write them in the spaces below and find something we should remember!

___'s _________

_____ __ __

__ ______

ANSWER: God's greatest gift to us is Jesus.

Round 'n' Round!

Start here!

Write the letters below and find something God wants us to do.

ANSWER: We are to share God's good news with all the world.

WORK THIS!

L	N	E	D	R
4+6=___	7+4=___	9-2=___	8-7=___	5+8=___

H	O	U	B	C
5-2=___	3×3=___	8-6=___	3×4=___	9-5=___

A	G	T
10-4=___	5+2+1=___	8-3=___

YOU CAN DO IT!

Use the math answers to find where to put the letters below:

Our ___ ___ ___ ___ ___ ___
4 3 2 13 4 3

helps us to

___ ___ ___ ___ ___ ___ ___ ___ ___ ___
10 7 6 13 11 6 12 9 2 5

___ ___ ___
8 9 1

ANSWER: Our church helps us to learn about God.

Round 'n' Round!

Start here!
O S H A R E G
T I T H A O
W O R L D
E S W D L S
R W E L G
A E H T O
E W N D O O

Write the letters below and find something God wants us to do.

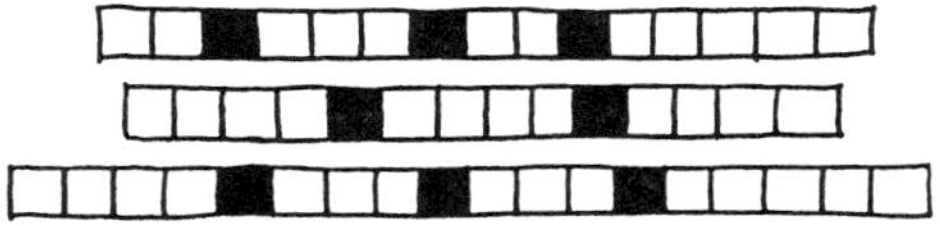

ANSWER: We are to share God's good news with all the world.

WORK THIS!

L	N	E	D	R
4+6= ___	7+4= ___	9-2= ___	8-7= ___	5+8= ___
H	**O**	**U**	**B**	**C**
5-2= ___	3×3= ___	8-6= ___	3×4= ___	9-5= ___
		A	**G**	**T**
		10-4= ___	5+2+1= ___	8-3= ___

YOU CAN DO IT!

Use the math answers to find where to put the letters below:

Our _ _ _ _ _ _ (4 3 2 13 4 3)

helps us to

_ _ _ _ _ (10 7 6 13 11) _ _ _ _ _ (6 12 9 2 5)

_ _ _ (8 9 1)

ANSWER: Our church helps us to learn about God.

AN EASTER TRUTH!

Use this code to put the correct letters in the spaces below:

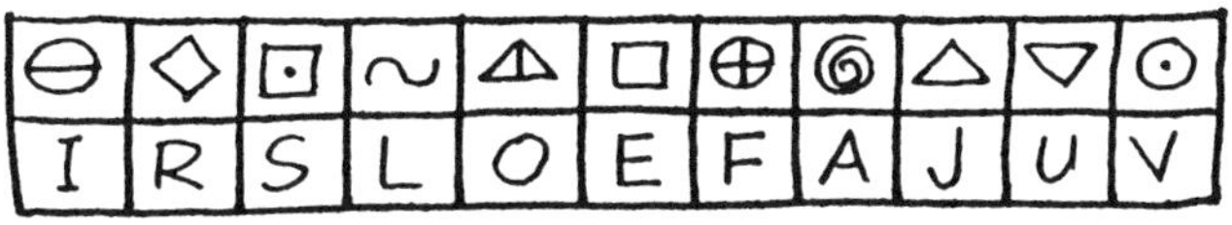
I R S L O E F A J U V

ANSWER: Jesus is alive forever.

RUN AROUND THE RING!
The letters in the circle will fill in the blanks below.
But you must cross out each B, M and Q that you come to!
START
G M O D C Q A N U S E U S C W H I L B D Q R E M N I B N Q H M I S B W O M R K

ANSWER: God can use us children in His work.

AN EASTER TRUTH!

Use this code to put the correct letters in the spaces below:

⊖	◇	⊡	∼	⟁	□	⊕	◎	△	▽	⊙
I	R	S	L	O	E	F	A	J	U	V

ANSWER: Jesus is alive forever.

RUN AROUND THE RING!
The letters in the circle will fill in the blanks below.
But you must cross out each B, M and Q that you come to!
START
G M O D C Q A N U S E U S C M H I L B D Q R E M W N I B N Q H M I S B W O M R K

ANSWER: God can use us children in His work.

BACK and FORTH!

L 1.
O 2.
V 3.
E 4.
O 5.
T 6.
H 7.
E 8.
R 9.
S 10.
R 11.
U 12.
D 13.
E 14.
U 15.
N 16.
K 17.
I 18.
N 19.
D 20.
FIND THE MESSAGE! PUT THE LETTERS ABOVE IN THE NUMBERED SPACES BELOW
Paris

God wants us to ____ (1 2 3 4) ______ (5 6 7 8 9 10)
even if they are
____ (11 12 13 14) or ______ (15 16 17 18 19 20)

ANSWER: God wants us to love others even if they are rude or unkind.

This is important!

All of us

OFFE KFTVT

BT TBWJPS

Use the alphabet to fill in the spaces below with the letter that comes just <u>before</u> each letter on the poster. For instance, if you came to a "C" you would put a "B."

ABCDEFGHIJKLM
NOPQRSTUVWXYZ

All of us ____ _____

__ ______

ANSWER: All of us need Jesus as Savior.

BACK and FORTH!

L 1. V 3. O 5. H 7. R 9. R 11. D 13. U 15. K 17. N 19.
O 2. E 4. T 6. E 8. S 10. U 12. E 14. N 16. I 18. D 20.
FIND THE MESSAGE! PUT THE LETTERS ABOVE IN THE NUMBERED SPACES BELOW

God wants us to _ _ _ _ (1 2 3 4) _ _ _ _ _ _ (5 6 7 8 9 10)

even if they are

_ _ _ _ (11 12 13 14) or _ _ _ _ _ _ (15 16 17 18 19 20)

ANSWER: God wants us to love others even if they are rude or unkind.

This is important!
All of us
OFFE KFTVT
BT TBWJPS
Use the alphabet to fill in the spaces below with the letter that comes just before each letter on the poster. For instance, if you came to a "C" you would put a "B."

A B C D E F G H I J K L M
N O P Q R S T U V W X Y Z

All of us _ _ _ _ _ _ _ _ _

_ _ _ _ _ _ _ _ _

ANSWER: All of us need Jesus as Savior.

Thank You!

Outline the shapes of the words and then match them with the word-shapes below
who
thanks
help
say
us
to
those
Jesus wants us to

ANSWER: Jesus wants us to say thanks to those who help us.

Remember...
We should use our
to
To work the puzzle, put each letter with its matching pattern

ANSWER: We should use our money to please God.

Thank You!

Outline the shapes of the words and then match them with the word-shapes below
who
thanks
help
say
us
to
those
Jesus wants us to

ANSWER: Jesus wants us to say thanks to those who help us.

Remember...

We should use our
to
To work the puzzle, put each letter with its matching pattern
y n s l p d e e m o G a

ANSWER: We should use our money to please God.

All Mixed Up!

teaches
His
loves
us
Jesus
The
that
sent
God
Bible
son
us
and
?
Fit the words
into the correct
spaces below.
T

ANSWER: The Bible teaches us that God loves us and sent His son Jesus.

All Mixed Up!

us
teaches
His
loves
Jesus
The
that
sent
God
Bible
son
us
and
?
Fit the words into the correct spaces below.
T

ANSWER: The Bible teaches us that God loves us and sent His son Jesus.

One-Two-Three!

with 7
10 will
11 give
I 5
6 am
strength 13
9 I
12 you
for 4
2 be
15 help
14 and
8 you
16 you
3 afraid
1 Don't
OH! I GET IT!
Connect the numbers, in order, with a line. Write each word on the matching line below.
GOD SAYS:
1 2 3 , 4
5 6 7 8 ; 9 10
11 12 13
14 15 16
ISAIAH 41:10

ANSWER: Don't be afraid, for I am with you; I will give you strength and help you.

Find the Message!

ZWQESVHOYULDVREQMEZMBEQ
RJVEQSUSCAYRESWHVENZ
QWEAVRZEYSIQCKORHVURZT

The hidden words above will fit into the spaces below. But you must cross out each Q, V, Y and Z that you come to!

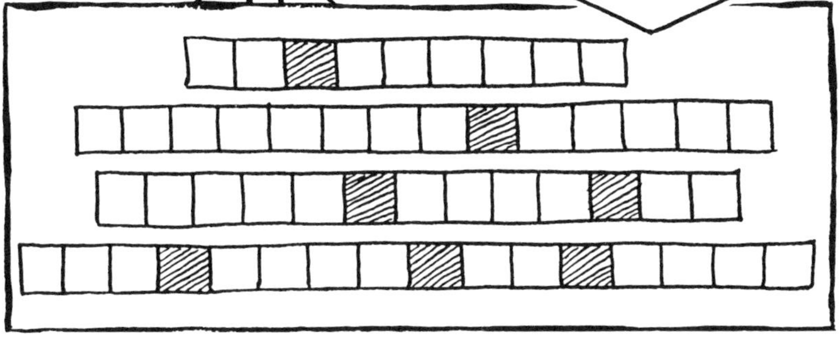

ANSWER: We should remember Jesus cares when we are sick or hurt.

MESSAGE from the SKY!
GAOBDIS
1
RDUELFEGS
2
AHRIE
3
FJOKR
4
OLUMR
5
ONWON
6
GPOQORD
7
Start with the first letter, jump one and take the next, through each group. Put them in the blocks below.

ANSWER: God's rules are for our own good.

Find the Message!

ZWQESVHOYULDVREQMEZMBEQ
RJVEQSUSCAYRESWHVENZ
QWEAVRZEYSIQCKORHVURZT

The hidden words above will fit into the spaces below. But you must cross out each Q, V, Y and Z that you come to!

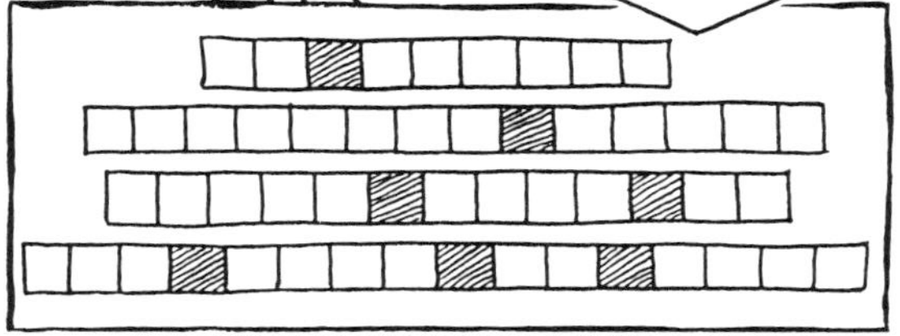

ANSWER: We should remember Jesus cares when we are sick or hurt.

MESSAGE from the SKY!

GAOBDIS ①
RDUELFEGS ②
AHRIE ③
FJOKR ④
OLUMR ⑤
ONWON ⑥
GPOQORD ⑦

Start with the first letter, jump one and take the next, through each group. Put them in the blocks below.

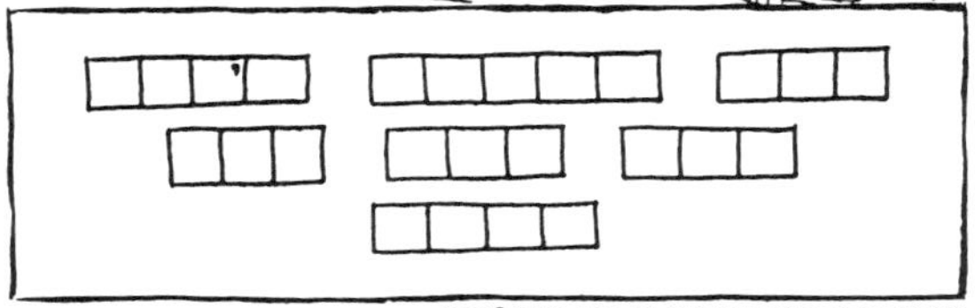

ANSWER: God's rules are for our own good.

Think On This!

D O I O O
O G E F T
S H L O N
R D E T T
R S A E I
H K H V G
Start
GO THE WAY THE ARROWS POINT AND PRINT THE LETTERS IN THE BLANKS BELOW!
Psalm 136:1
Paris

ANSWER: Give thanks to the Lord for He is good.

Write On!

HAN
KYO
UGO
DFO
RAL
LTHO
SEW
HOH
ELPU
SLE
ARN

Starting at left, write all the letters above in the boxes below. They will form a special prayer for you.

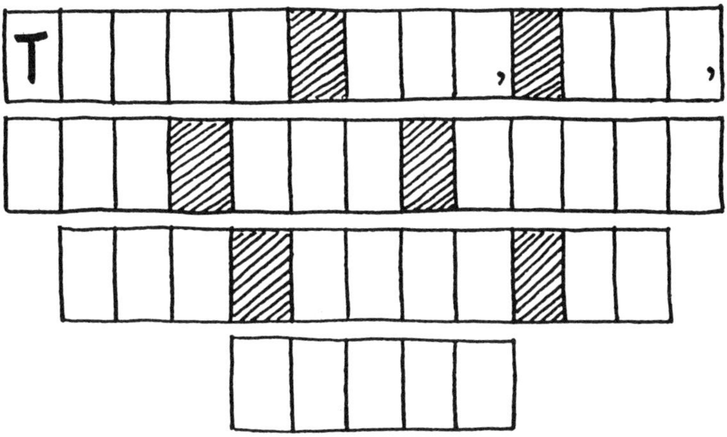
T

ANSWER: Thank you, God, for all those who help us learn.

Think On This!

D O I O O
O G E F T
S H L O N
R D E T T
R S A E I
H K H V G
Start
GO THE WAY THE ARROWS POINT AND PRINT THE LETTERS IN THE BLANKS BELOW!
Psalm 136:1

ANSWER: Give thanks to the Lord for He is good.

Write On!

HAN
KYO
UGO
DFO
RAL
LTHO
SEW
HOH
ELPU
SLE
ARN

Starting at left, write all the letters above in the boxes below. They will form a special prayer for you.

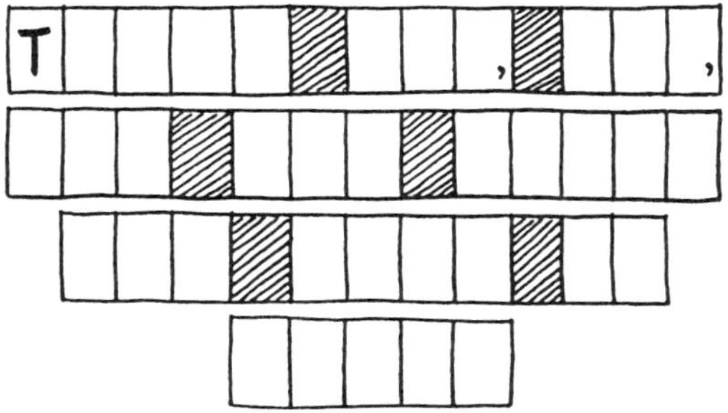
T

ANSWER: Thank you, God, for all those who help us learn.

In the Circle!

Jesus wants me to be friendly and...

15 3 14 8 5 1 3
5 2 6 3 11 10
7 13 2 5
1 9
4 8 2 7 12 7 2 7 3 10

Match the numbers to the letters and fill them in!

1 = M	4 = A	7 = I	10 = S	13 = N
2 = T	5 = O	8 = C	11 = R	14 = L
3 = E	6 = H	9 = Y	12 = V	15 = W

ANSWER: Welcome others into my activities.

DO THIS!
START AT THE LOWEST BALLOON AND FILL IN THE BLANKS BELOW AS YOU GO AROUND
Jesus wants us to ______ ___ ______ and ______
Paris

ANSWER: Jesus wants us to honor our mother and father.

In the Circle!

Jesus wants me to be friendly and...

15 3 14 8 5 1 3
5 2 6 3 11 10
7 13 2 5
1 9
4 8 2 7 12 7 2 7 3 10

Match the numbers to the letters and fill them in!

1 = M	4 = A	7 = I	10 = S	13 = N
2 = T	5 = O	8 = C	11 = R	14 = L
3 = E	6 = H	9 = Y	12 = V	15 = W

ANSWER: Welcome others into my activities.

O U R M O T H E R A N D F A T H E R O N O H

DO THIS!

START AT THE LOWEST BALLOON AND FILL IN THE BLANKS BELOW AS YOU GO AROUND

Jesus wants us to _ _ _ _ _ _ _ _

_ _ _ _ _ _ and

_ _ _ _ _ _

ANSWER: Jesus wants us to honor our mother and father.

Guess What!
T S P R I M
N U G A H
START
A S N I O
G W T I S T
O D O S E S
Follow the arrows down, up, and down and write the letters below

ANSWER: God wants us to sing praises to Him.

DID YOU KNOW THIS?

God
loves
3.
7 1 4 4 10 6 2 8
9 5 11 4 10
2 Cor. 9:7

First, work the math. The answers will tell you where to fill in the letters.

I. 10−5= ___	E. 1+2+1= ___
G. 2+5+2= ___	V. 2×6−1= ___
A. 8−5= ___	H. 9−8= ___
R. 5×2= ___	F. 3+2+1= ___
L. 11−3= ___	C. 2+2+3= ___

U. 2×4−6= ___

ANSWER: God loves a cheerful giver.

Guess What!
T S P R I M
N U G A H
START A S N I O
G W T I S T
O D O S E S
Follow the arrows down, up, and down and write the letters below

ANSWER: God wants us to sing praises to Him.

DID YOU KNOW THIS?
God loves
3.
7 1 4 4 10 6 2 8
9 5 11 4 10
2 Cor. 9:7
First, work the math. The answers will tell you where to fill in the letters.
I. 10-5= ___
G. 2+5+2= ___
A. 8-5 = ___
R. 5×2 = ___
L. 11-3 = ___
E. 1+2+1= ___
V. 2×6-1= ___
H. 9-8 = ___
F. 3+2+1= ___
C. 2+2+3= ___
U. 2×4-6= ___

ANSWER: God loves a cheerful giver.

Got It?
Use the code to match the letters with the boxes below!
S...
F..-.
R.-.
E.
A.-
O---
L.-..
U..-
I..
H....
C-.-.
N-.
T-
Jesus wants us to be
and
He does not want us to
or

ANSWER: Jesus wants us to be truthful and honest. He does not want us to lie or cheat.

This Is God's Earth!
USE THIS SECRET CODE
to fill in the words below
U I K B N D R F
T L A E O S P

ANSWER: Don't litter. Let's keep it beautiful.

Got It?
Use the code to match the letters with the boxes below!
S...
F....
R...
E.
A._
O._
L....
U..._
I..
H....
C.....
T_
N_.
Jesus wants us to be
and
He does not want us to
or

ANSWER: Jesus wants us to be truthful and honest. He does not want us to lie or cheat.

This Is God's Earth!
USE THIS SECRET CODE to fill in the words below
U I K B N D R F
T L A E O S P

ANSWER: Don't litter. Let's keep it beautiful.

A Christmas Prayer

TKNAH
OUY
DGO
ROF
GSNNIDE
SUJSE
H
S
U
Solve the puzzle by putting the jumbled letters into their correct order.
Paris

ANSWER: Thank you, God, for sending Jesus.

Unlock This Message!

G⊟ds⊟l⊟v⧄dth
⧄w⊟rldth⊙th⧄
g⊙v⧄t⊟⊕sh▽s⊟
nlys⊟n
HERE'S THE KEY!
⊙=A ⧄=E
▽=I ⊟=O ⊕=U
Write all the words below.

ANSWER: God so loved the world that He gave to us His only Son.

A Christmas Prayer

TKNAH
OUY
DGO
ROF
GSNNIDE
SUJSE
H
S
U
Solve the puzzle by putting the jumbled letters into their correct order.

ANSWER: Thank you, God, for sending Jesus.

Unlock This Message!

HERE'S THE KEY!
write all the words below.

ANSWER: God so loved the world that He gave to us His only Son.

A Thanksgiving Thought

Let your pencil help you find a Thanksgiving prayer. Don't cross any lines!

Thank You, God, for all our many blessings

TRACK THIS!

- what ⧄
- and ▷
- doers ⊕
- not □
- God △
- of ◁
- just ⊖
- says ◫
- hearers ▽

Here's how!

Match the words on the signs with their marks below.

We should be

______ ⊕ ______ ◁ ______ ⧄

______ △ ______ ◫ ______ ▷

______ □ ______ ⊖

______ ▽

ANSWER: We should be doers of what God says and not just hearers.

A Thanksgiving Thought

Let your pencil help you find a Thanksgiving prayer. Don't cross any lines!

Thank You, God, for all our many blessings

Track This!

and
doers
not
what
God
just
of
says
hearers

Here's how!

Match the words on the signs with their marks below.

We should be

___ ⊕ ___ ◁ ___ ⊠

___ △ ___ ◫ ___ ▷

___ □ ___ ⊖

___ ▽

ANSWER: We should be doers of what God says and not just hearers.

Fill It In!
Use a pencil or crayon to fill in every space with a dot in it. The hidden words will complete the blanks below.
We should all ☐☐☐☐ ☐☐☐☐☐☐ in need
Paris

ANSWER: We should all help others in need.

KNOCK OUT the NO-NOs!

W G O J D B K E W E J P S H B
I S J P R W O M B I J S E W B S
The correct letters from above will fill the blanks below and tell a great truth.
But the secret is you must leave out each B, J, and W that you come to!
Paris

ANSWER: God keeps His promises.

Fill It In!

Use a pencil or crayon to fill in every space with a dot in it. The hidden words will complete the blanks below.
We should all ☐☐☐☐ ☐☐☐☐☐☐ in need

ANSWER: We should all help others in need.

KNOCK OUT the NO-NOs!

W G O J D B K E W E J P S H B
I S J P R W O M B I J S E W B S
The correct letters from above will fill the blanks below and tell a great truth. But the secret is you must leave out each B, J, and W that you come to!

ANSWER: God keeps His promises.

WORDS on the WING

TO
3+2=__
FAITHFUL
4+3=__
WILL
6-4=__
US
7-3=__
BE
5+1=__
GOD
9-8=__
HELP
2+1=__
Paris

The math answers above will help you put the words in their right order below. Write them in!

1. ________
2. ________
3. ________
4. ________
5. ________
6. ________
7. ________

ANSWER: God will help us to be faithful.

A PRAYER FOR
The Fourth of July!
T
Match the drawings below with the same drawings above. This will give you the correct letters to spell out a special thought.
S
U
R
B
L
E
C
G
D
Y
O
N

ANSWER: God bless our country.

WORDS on the WING
TO
3+2= __
FAITHFUL
4+3= __
WILL
6–4= __
US
7–3= __
BE
5+1= __
GOD
9–8= __
HELP
2+1= __
The math answers above will help you put the words in their right order below. Write them in!
1.
2.
3.
4.
5.
6.
7.

ANSWER: God will help us to be faithful.

Break the Balloons!
Love
Sharing
Anger
Unkind words
Selfishness
Giving
Uncaring
Kindness
Helping others
Cross out the words that show what God does not like. The other words show what God does like. Write them here:
Paris

ANSWER: love, sharing, giving, kindness, helping others

Where's the Verse?

C F A R O B R A L G L E I
V A S E A T W N A L D K Y
H O U O R W S E I B A L T
L R I B D P E A T I F E O
R G L A I U G V H E A R N
HERE'S WHAT TO DO!
Put each numbered letter above into the blank below that has the same number.
Luke 6:37

ANSWER: Forgive, and you will be forgiven.

Break the Balloons!

Love
Sharing
Anger
Selfishness
Unkind words
Giving
Uncaring
Kindness
Helping others

Cross out the words that show what God does not like. The other words show what God <u>does</u> like. Write them here:

______________ ______________

______________ ______________

____

ANSWER: love, sharing, giving, kindness, helping others

Where's the Verse?

C	F 1	A	R	O 2	B	R 3	A	L	G 4	L	E	I 5
V 6	A	S	E 7	A 8	T	W	N 9	A	L	D 10	K	Y 11
H	O 12	U 13	O	R	W 14	S	E	I 15	B	A	L 16	T
L 17	R	I	B 18	D	P	E 19	A	T	I	F 20	E	O 21
R 22	G 23	L	A	I 24	U	G	V 25	H	E 26	A	R	N 27

HERE'S WHAT TO DO!

Put each numbered letter above into the blank <u>below</u> that has the same number.

__ __ __ __ __ __ __ , __ __ __
1 2 3 4 5 6 7 , 8 9 10

__ __ __   __ __ __ __   __ __
11 12 13   14 15 16 17   18 19

__ __ __ __ __ __ __ __
20 21 22 23 24 25 26 27

Luke 6:37

ANSWER: Forgive, and you will be forgiven.